You Are What
You Believe

YOU ARE WHAT YOU BELIEVE

Simple Steps to Transform Your Life

Hyrum W. Smith

Berrett–Koehler Publishers, Inc.
a BK Life book

Berrett-Koehler Publishers, Inc.

1333 Broadway, Suite 1000

Oakland, CA 94612-1921

Tel: (510) 817-2277   Fax: (510) 817-2278   www.bkconnection.com

Ordering Information

Quantity sales. Special discounts are available on quantity purchases by corporations, associations, and others. For details, contact the "Special Sales Department" at the Berrett-Koehler address above.

Individual sales. Berrett-Koehler publications are available through most bookstores. They can also be ordered directly from Berrett-Koehler: Tel: (800) 929-2929; Fax: (802) 864-7626; www.bkconnection.com

Orders for college textbook/course adoption use. Please contact Berrett-Koehler: Tel: (800) 929-2929; Fax: (802) 864-7626.

Orders by U.S. trade bookstores and wholesalers. Please contact Ingram Publisher Services, Tel: (800) 509-4887; Fax: (800) 838-1149; E-mail: customer .service@ingrampublisherservices.com; or visit www.ingrampublisherservices .com/Ordering for details about electronic ordering.

Berrett-Koehler and the BK logo are registered trademarks of Berrett-Koehler Publishers, Inc.

Printed in the United States of America

Berrett-Koehler books are printed on long-lasting acid-free paper. When it is available, we choose paper that has been manufactured by environmentally responsible processes. These may include using trees grown in sustainable forests, incorporating recycled paper, minimizing chlorine in bleaching, or recycling the energy produced at the paper mill.

Library of Congress Cataloging-in-Publication Data

Names: Smith, Hyrum W., author.
Title: You are what you believe : simple steps to transform your life / Hyrum W. Smith.
Description: Oakland, CA : Berrett-Koehler Publishers, [2016]
Identifiers: LCCN 2016012213 | ISBN 9781626566668 (pbk.)
Subjects: LCSH: Conduct of life. | Values. | Self-esteem. | Attitude (Psychology) | Change (Psychology)
Classification: LCC BJ1589 .S6474 2016 | DDC 170/.44—dc23
LC record available at https://lccn.loc.gov/2016012213

First Edition

20 19 18 17 16   10 9 8 7 6 5 4 3 2 1

Cover designer: Nancy Austin

DEDICATION

I am quite sure that each of us has someone, or a few people, in our lives who have made a significant contribution to making us who we are today. These are often teachers, coaches, parents, siblings, childhood friends, colleagues at work, religious leaders, or just plain folks who have been there at a crucial time in our lives and pointed us in the right direction.

One of those great human beings for me is a man named Jerry Pulsipher. Our paths first crossed in 1962 and again in 1963 in London, England. Since that time we have worked together on many projects, and he has helped me write several books. He was one of the team members that discovered the Reality Model and helped me to discover its power.

This book is dedicated to him. William Watson said it best:

> 'Tis human fortune's happiest height to be
> A spirit melodious, lucid, poised and whole.
> Second in order of felicity
> I hold it, to have walk'd with such a soul.

Jerry is a great and noble soul, one without whom this book would not exist. Thank you, Jerry, for leading the way for me.

CONTENTS

FOREWORD

I met Hyrum Smith over thirty years ago when we shared the speaking platform as part of a daylong seminar on executive excellence. We immediately became soul mates when we discovered our mutual belief that effective living and leading is a result of mastering a few simple truths. As a result, throughout our careers we have strived to identify some of those simple truths to help ourselves and others live better lives. That's what *The One Minute Manager*—as well as, I hope, all of my follow-up books—were all about.

Helping people make their lives work was certainly Hyrum's intention when he and his colleagues created the Franklin Planner and time management seminars. He and his fabulous wife Gail started Franklin Quest and later, through acquisition, created Franklin Covey.

As good as those concepts were, it is my opinion that Hyrum's greatest work began when he and Jerry Pulsipher developed the Reality Model—the core concept of this wonderful book. I first heard Hyrum speak about the Reality Model over twenty years ago when he agreed to be the "cleanup" speaker on a national tour I was doing with Don Shula, the legendary coach of the undefeated 1972 Miami Dolphins football team, to promote our coauthored book *Everyone's a Coach*. Don and I would talk about the simple truths in our book and then turn the microphone over to

Hyrum, who would help the audience understand how to apply the book's concepts to their lives. Enter the Reality Model and its own simple truth: effective living starts and ends with our beliefs about how to satisfy our basic needs. When Hyrum said, "You are what you believe," people's eyes lit up. And, to be honest, Hyrum got the highest ratings of any of us as a speaker. That's why I'm so excited that this book is being made available.

The big idea of the book is this: if you're not getting what you want in a certain part of your life, you can always trace it to a lousy belief. It was fun to watch Don Shula listen to Hyrum tell his favorite stories—stories like the man who was on his fourth marriage and had a strong belief that men were superior to women! Was that belief working for him in marriage? Duh! Don would roar with laughter every time.

Hyrum's Reality Model really helped me a few years ago when I found myself tipping the scale at more than thirty pounds over my normal weight. One day my wife Margie asked me what my philosophy of eating was—particularly when I was on the road, consulting and teaching. I answered, "If I've been working hard, I deserve to eat anything I want at night." She said, "So, how's that working for you?" I realized if I wanted to change the results I was getting, I needed to change my belief. The use of Hyrum's Reality Model was instrumental in helping me turn my health around, which resulted in my writing *Fit at Last: Look and Feel Better Once and for All* with my fitness coach, Tim Kearin.

Read *You Are What You Believe* and change the results you're getting in an area of your life that's not working. Thanks, Hyrum, for sharing the simple truths inherent in your Reality Model. It will continue to make a difference in my life and in the lives of all the people who are fortunate enough to be reading this book, as well as the family members and friends with whom they share it.

Ken Blanchard, coauthor,
The One Minute Manager and *Refire! Don't Retire*

PREFACE

Back in the late 1980s the Franklin Quest company was growing at a meteoric pace. Franklin Planners began to appear all over the world. The planner and the time management seminar that went with it were creating remarkable and lasting change in those we taught.

Over 90 percent of the people who began using the Franklin Planner would purchase the refill every year. As a result, we became obsessed with the answer to the question, "Why do they do that?" Then came the real question: "What causes permanent behavioral change?" As we continued to ask ourselves that question, we discovered the Reality Model.

We didn't call it the Reality Model at first; it was just a visual way of describing what was going on in people's lives anyway. Jerry Pulsipher, to whom this book is dedicated, led the way in this discovery. None of us ever talked about creating the model or even inventing the model; it was always, "We *discovered* the model."

I was so taken by the model's potential for good that I began giving what I call my You Are What You Believe speech all over the world. In the late 1980s I was asked to present this speech at the Securities Industry Institute's annual school held at the Wharton School of Business in Philadelphia. And for the last twenty-seven years I have been invited back to make the same speech to each new class. The reception of the speech has been so positive that we decided to turn it into a book.

So here it is. If you want to know why you do what you do, and how to make changes that last forever, this book is for you. When you have finished reading *You Are What You Believe* you will likely want to invest in a large bottle of Windex.

||||||||||||||||||||||||||||||||||||||||||||||||||||||||||||||||||||||||||||||||||||||||||||||

THE REALITY MODEL PROMISE

First, I want you to know that I take your commitment to reading this book very seriously. I know the impact that adhering to the principles in this book can make in your life, so I'm going to ask you to do three things as you read.

1. Take notes. Write down or highlight everything that resonates with you.
2. When you have finished the book, take the next thirty-six hours to review, ponder, and consider the notes you've taken. Just think about them.
3. Within forty-eight hours of finishing this book, teach what you have learned to one other person. This can be a spouse, friend, neighbor, associate, teenager, or someone on the bus.

If you'll do these three things, I will *guarantee* that you will see a marked and measurable change in how you make personal and professional decisions. Now, that's a big promise to make before you've read anything, but I've had the opportunity to share this with a lot of people around the world. I'm very confident about what this book can accomplish if you'll do those three things. Do we have a deal? Then read on.

||||||||||||||||||||||||||||||||||||||||||||||||||||||||||||||||||||||||||||||||||||||||||||

CHAPTER 1

BEHAVIOR CHANGE

There are three constants in life: change, choice, and
principles.

—ATTRIBUTED TO DR. STEPHEN R. COVEY

Basic Principles of Productivity

Think about the following statement:

> The basic principles that help a human being
> become more productive and effective have
> not changed for six thousand years.

Thirty-three years ago I started the Franklin Planner
business with my partners. Since then I have had the opportunity to teach a great number of time management
seminars all over the world. Through the years it has become common for people to approach me before or after a
presentation. They come up to me, lower their voices, look
around to make sure nobody's listening, and then say, "You
know, Hyrum, I wish I lived a hundred years ago, when they
had more time."

"Really?" I'd respond. "How much more time did they
have a hundred years ago?"

"Oh, they had a lot more time."

That is a common misperception. Do you know what the only difference is between today and a hundred years ago? It is that today we have more options. Why do we have more options? Because we do things faster. As a technologically advanced culture, we are into speed.

If my grandfather missed a train, it was no big deal. He'd wait twenty-four hours and catch another train. If my father missed an airplane, it was no big deal. He'd wait five hours and catch another airplane. If I miss one section of a revolving door, I go nuts. And so do you. Why do we do that? Because we want speed, that's why. Would you tolerate today the speed of a computer from fifteen years ago?

> The basic principles that help a human being become more productive and effective have not changed for six thousand years.

Say it out loud. Write it down.

Every generation has to rediscover these principles. We give new names to them; we write books about them. A good friend of mine, Stephen Covey, wrote a book, *The 7 Habits of Highly Effective People*. I wrote a book, *What Matters Most*. Read either book. There's not a new idea in either book. Why do I tell you this? Because what I'm going to be sharing with you in this book is really old stuff; it just happens to be very relevant for today. The magic of the 7 Habits is the fact that Stephen put seven of them together. The magic is how they are taught for the twenty-first century. The basic principles go back a long way.

Why do I make an issue of this? What hasn't changed in the last hundred or a thousand years? You and I. As human beings, we haven't changed. We still have to go to the bathroom several times a day. We put our pants on one leg at a time. The human being is the same. What has changed? Our environment has changed. And it continues to change at warp speed. The tools with which we implement these principles are changing fast. But the basic principles that help you and me become better, greater people haven't changed for a long time.

The process of learning these principles must be rediscovered in every generation by individuals and organizations. We explored this at Franklin Quest, the time management company I founded back in the 1980s.

Understanding Permanent Behavior Change

As mentioned earlier, at Franklin Quest we became obsessed with this question: What causes permanent behavioral change? Carrying a planner around was a behavioral change. Why did six million people in 170 countries do that?

As we asked ourselves this question, a model surfaced that we all could agree upon. We decided to call it the Reality Model.

In this book I'm going to introduce you to the Reality Model, and make you dangerous with it. This model can, if you allow it to, change your life and the lives of all those with whom you share it. The foundation of the model is understanding the definitions of the "real world," principles, natural laws, and addiction.

The Real World Defined

The real world is the world as it *really* is, not as we *believe* it is or think it *should* be. This is an important definition to keep in mind. We will come back to it later.

After I left Franklin Covey, some friends and I started a new venture called the Galileo Initiative. Why did we call our new little venture Galileo? As I'm sure you know, Galileo was an Italian physicist, mathematician, astronomer, and philosopher who played a major role in the Scientific Revolution. His achievements include improvements to the telescope and the consequent astronomical observations, and he has been called the "father of science."

Until the time of Galileo, most people in the Western world believed that the earth was the center of the universe and the sun went around the earth. Actually, in the early sixteenth century, it was Copernicus who first stated that the earth revolved around the sun. He died in 1543, just twenty years before Galileo was born. With the exception of a few, no one took his theory seriously. Then Galileo came along and said, "Hey, I've improved the telescope! I've done the math! I can prove that the earth is going around the sun!"

How did the world react to this new concept? Galileo was ridiculed, put on trial, convicted of heresy, and excommunicated from the church. He spent the last fifteen years of his life under house arrest, as a condemned heretic. But . . . he was right. He had the correct perception of the real world. That's what the Reality Model helps us do: it helps us to see the world as it really is.

Before we get into the nuts and bolts of the Reality Model, I would like to define three more words that will be used in our discussion.

Principles

Once we see how things really are, we begin to perceive the principles our beliefs are based upon. *Principles are what we believe to be true about ourselves, and what we believe about the world and our place in it.* The principles we follow don't change based on how our outside circumstances influence us. Correct principles can give us direction as we make life decisions. They are guideposts that help us successfully navigate the bombardment of change we are experiencing every day.

Natural Laws

Natural laws are fundamental patterns of nature and life that human experience has shown to be valid. Natural laws are rarely if ever changed or influenced to move in a different direction. We cannot change these laws to be what we want because they are universal and affect everyone. Choosing to accept or reject these laws will have an impact on the choices we make and the consequences of those choices.

Addiction

Here is my definition: *addiction is compulsive behavior with short-term benefits and long-term destruction.* This is not a book on addiction, and this is not a dictionary definition of addiction, but the purpose of my definition will become evident as you continue.

When I say the word *addiction*, most people start thinking about drugs and alcohol. Abusing these substances does in fact represent addictive behavior. But alcoholism and drug abuse are only two of many different kinds of addictive behaviors. Think about other kinds of addictive behaviors: exercising too much, working too hard, and overeating, among others! There are many different addictive behaviors.

Now that we have defined the real world, principles, natural laws, and addictions, you are ready to be introduced to the Reality Model. As you read, remember these definitions. They will be instrumental in understanding and applying the model effectively.

||||||||||||||||||||||||||||||||||||||||||||||||||||||||||||||||||||||||||||||||||||||||||||||||||||

CHAPTER 2

THE REALITY MODEL

*Beliefs have the power to create and the power to
destroy. Human beings have the awesome ability to take
any experience of their lives and create a meaning that
disempowers them or one that can literally save their
lives.*

—ANTHONY ROBBINS, *AWAKEN THE GIANT WITHIN*

For now, mentally shelve the definitions given in chapter 1. Go back and review them if you have to. Here is a
representation of the Reality Model, without labels. As you
read what each figure represents, think about the flow of
the model, and how the five pieces relate to each other.

Human Needs

Let's start with the first part of the model: Human Needs.
Now, understand this fact: you have four powerful, driving
needs. Whether you think you've got them or not, you've got
them. Psychologists have done all kinds of studies, and
many agree that we have at least these four needs:

Human Needs

I. The need to live.
2. The need to love and be loved.
3. The need to feel important, to have value and significance.
4. The need to have variety in our lives.

The most interesting one to me, by the way, is the fact that we all have a need for variety. That's why you have a closet full of different kinds of clothes, you go on vacations, and you pay for cable or satellite TV to watch a wide range of shows and productions. We have a very strong need for variety.

We represent the first piece of our model with a wheel because this is the piece that drives the model. You may even label this wheel with the word *engine* because this is where the model gets its power.

The Belief Window

The second piece of the model is the Belief Window. Inside that window is the word *Principles*.

Belief Window

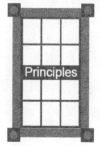

You have a Belief Window. It sits in front of your face. Imagine that a wire comes from the back of your head across the top and hooks onto that window. Every time you move your head, the window moves with you. You look out into the world through this window; you accept information from the world through this window. On this window you have placed thousands of principles that you have accepted as correct.

The minute I say the word *principles*, a lot of people start thinking about heavy-duty religious stuff. It's true that religious and ethical principles may be on your Belief Window, but there are thousands of tiny little principles as well. We put principles on our Belief Window because we believe they'll help us satisfy the four Human Needs. The number of principles you have on your Belief Window is a function of your age; the older you are, the more principles you will have on it.

An example of a principle you might have on your Belief Window might be something like this: "All Doberman pinschers are vicious."

Which of the four Human Needs is driving this principle? It clearly has something to do with the need to live.

Somewhere in your life, you decided to accept the idea that Doberman pinschers are vicious as a correct principle. You believe it, so you put that principle on your Belief Window.

If-Then Rules

The third piece of the model looks like a little bridge. On top of that bridge is the word *Rules*. Inside that bridge are two tiny words: *If* and *Then*.

This is how the Belief Window works: the minute you put a principle on your Belief Window, you immediately start to create rules that will govern your behavior based upon that principle. This all goes on in your head at the speed of light. You do it automatically, and sometimes even without realizing which principles you are actually putting on your Belief Window.

I call these If-Then Rules. Let's say that you do have the principle on your Belief Window that all Doberman pinschers are vicious; you have accepted this as a correct principle. So *if* you encounter a big Doberman pinscher, *then* what will you do? You will leap tall buildings with a single bound. You will run away. You will have a very specific set of rules all set up based on that principle on your Belief Window.

It is important to understand that first three pieces of this model are all invisible. You can't see the process. No one else can see it. But it's going on, every second you breathe.

Behavior Patterns

Let's go to the fourth piece of the Reality Model, which is a right-facing triangle. Down the slope on the top of that triangle is the word *Behavior.* Inside the triangle is the word *Action.*

Let's go back to that same principle: all Doberman pinschers are vicious. If that's true, then we set up our rules. Rules are automatic. If you go in somebody's yard and there's a Doberman, what behavior pattern will we see? You will perform the same action every single time.

Let's take another principle through the model to this point. Here is a principle: "My self-worth is dependent on my possessions." Do you know anyone who has that principle on his or her Belief Window? Which of the four Human Needs would drive this principle? The need to feel important, for sure. Anything else?

Let's pretend I have a second principle on my Belief Window: European stuff is better than American stuff. Now I have two principles on my Belief Window: (1) my self-worth is dependent on my stuff, and (2) European stuff is better.

Let's take that through the model. If that's true, the rules we set up will reflect those beliefs. It's now time for me to buy a car. What kind of car will I buy? What kind of clothes will I wear? Both will be European, of course. And I am likely not going to feel good about myself without that car or those clothes.

Let me tell you a story to illustrate how Belief Windows can be passed on from generation to generation. One Sunday morning a man comes into his kitchen and notices his wife is cooking a wonderful dinner. As she pulls a beautifully cooked ham from the oven, he notices that the ends have been removed from it. He is curious, so he asks his wife, "Why did you cut the ends off the ham?"

"It makes it taste better," she says.

"How do you know that?"

"My mother taught me that."

On this woman's Belief Window is the principle that if you cut the ends off the ham it makes it taste better. (We know she believes that, because that is what she has done.) The man is really curious because he has never seen his own mother do that. The next Sunday he's at the in-laws' house for dinner. He takes his mother-in-law aside and says, "I understand you cut the ends off your ham."

"I do."

"Why do you do that?"

"It makes it taste better."

"How do you know that?"

"My mother taught me that."

Two generations of women now have the same principle on their Belief Window: cutting the ends off the ham makes it taste better. But the man doesn't understand this logic. The grandmother is still alive at age ninety-three, so he calls her on the phone.

"I understand you cut the ends off your ham."

"I do."

"Why do you do that?"

"Won't fit in the oven if I don't."

Here was a practical reason as the origin of the practice, but two generations later, the principle or belief floats down on a Belief Window: cutting the ends off the ham makes it taste better.

Results and Feedback

Look at the last piece of the model. The final piece in the model is a little box. Above the box is the word *Results*.

Results allow us to examine current principles on our Belief Window. If we don't like the results we are getting, *we can move back through the model to see what principles on our Belief Window are causing these results*. There is a line labeled *Feedback* connecting the *Results* box with the Human Needs wheel. Results are linked with the needs that everyone has. Whatever behavior we exhibit, it is ultimately an attempt to fulfill one or more of those Human Needs. The results of this behavior will determine whether or not we have successfully met our Human Needs.

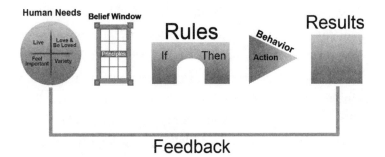

Needs and Natural Laws

Throughout this book I am going to introduce you to seven natural laws. If you will commit these seven laws to memory, the impact on your personal and professional decision-making process will amaze you. Let's look at the first two natural laws and then run some principles through the model.

> The first natural law: If the results of your behavior do not meet your needs, there is an incorrect principle or belief on your Belief Window.
>
> The second natural law: Results take time to measure.

Let's say that Gary has a principle on his Belief Window: "My self-worth is dependent on never losing an argument." If he believes that, then he sets up his rules. Rules are automatic. Gary gets in an argument with his fifteen-year-old son. What behavior pattern will we see? Gary will make sure that he wins every single time due to his belief that his self-worth is dependent on never losing an argument.

Now ask this question: Will the results of Gary's behavior meet his needs over time? Yes or no? If the answer is no, what does that mean about his Belief Window? It means that there is a negative and/or incorrect or incomplete principle on his Belief Window.

I'm going to give you another principle now, and let's take it all the way through the model. Here is the principle: "My self-worth is dependent on never losing at games." Do you know anyone who has that principle on his or her Belief Window?

Let's pretend that I have that belief on my Belief Window. Which of the four Human Needs is driving the belief that my self-worth is dependent on never losing at games? The need to feel important, for sure. If I believe that to be true, then I set up my rules: I'm not okay unless I win.

I now get in a game with someone, and I start to lose. What behavior pattern will you see from me?

I'll cheat.

And I'll do everything in my power to win. Now we've got to ask this question: Will the results of my behavior meet my needs over time? If the answer is no, what does that mean about my Belief Window? Is there an incorrect principle on my Belief Window?

Several years ago, on the front page of *USA Today* was a headline stating that one out of three CEOs cheat at golf. It was a long, detailed article. It told how they did it. So the reader now has to ask, If they'll fudge in a ten-dollar game of golf, what will they do in a million-dollar deal? This was right around the time Enron collapsed. What do you think was on the Belief Window of the people at Enron?

Okay, I'm going to walk a potentially controversial principle through the model. For the sake of discussion only, let's say that someone has on his or her Belief Window the principle that men are better than women. Do you know any men who have that principle on their Belief Windows? Do you know any women who have that principle on their Belief Windows? Which of the four Human Needs would drive a principle like that? The need to live? The need to feel important?

That actually was a prevalent belief in the world until about a hundred years ago. As a side note, one of the first debates Benjamin Franklin took part in as a young man was in defense of educating women in this country.

Franklin wrote in his autobiography, "John Collins was of the Opinion that it [educating women] was improper; and that they were naturally unequal to it. I took the contrary side."

Let's now continue through the model. I have the principle on my Belief Window that men are better than women. Saturday morning my wife says, "Hyrum, I have a lot of errands to run today, would you mind vacuuming the house while I'm gone?" Given what I believe, what behavior will you see from me? I might say, "I don't do that, that's women's work."

Now we have to ask this question: Will the results of my behavior meet my needs over time? Probably not. So what do we know about my Belief Window? I've got an incorrect principle on my Belief Window.

Where do we get principles for our Belief Windows? Where do they come from? Well, they start when we're pretty small. If a little girl in our society acts like a boy, what do we call her? A tomboy. That is okay in our culture. If a little boy acts like a girl, what do we call him? Some people call him a sissy. That's the nicest thing they call him. That's *not* okay in our culture.

Here's another story. A ten-year-old boy walks into his garage on a Saturday morning. While doing what kids do in a garage on Saturday mornings, he accidentally tips a box off the shelf and it lands on his foot. It smashes three toes, he bleeds all over the floor, and he starts to cry. Dad comes into the garage. What does his dad say to that little boy?

"Don't cry. Men don't cry."

"This hurts, I'd like to cry. Why can't I cry, Dad?"

"Because men don't cry."

Scientists tell us that tears exuded over an onion have a very different chemistry than tears exuded in anguish. We apparently get rid of some ugly toxins from our bodies when we cry. We don't allow men that privilege in our culture: "real" men don't cry.

Changing Principles and Beliefs Changes Behavior

Before any of my behavior will change, the principle on my Belief Window has to change. I have to find an alternative principle. What principle will likely work? Men and women are equal. They are different—wonderfully different—but equal.

If I get that principle on my Belief Window, will it alter my behavior? Yes, it will. Let's reexamine that earlier scenario. On a Saturday morning my wife says, "Hyrum, I've got a lot of errands to run today, would you mind vacuuming the house while I'm gone?" What kind of behavior do you think we will see next? "Sure. I'd be happy to!"

Individuals aren't the only ones to have Belief Windows; groups have them as well. Families have them, neighborhoods have them, cities have them, corporations have them, and nations have them.

I'm going to give you a principle now that we at Franklin Quest had on our corporate Belief Window in the beginning. I say "had" because we discovered that this was not a good principle. Ask yourself which of the four Human Needs was driving this principle, and let's take it through the model. Here was our principle: "Cut costs, no matter what."

That doesn't sound like a bad principle, does it? Which of the four Human Needs is in play? The need to live. In our case it felt like survival was driving it. Why would the needs of a corporation be identical to the needs of a human being? Corporations are made up of human beings.

So the principle on our Belief Window was "Cut costs, no matter what." Then we set up our rules. Of course, nobody sends a memo out saying, "Set your rules up." Rules are automatic. It's now time for us to hire a receptionist. What kind of receptionist will we hire? Based on our principle, we will hire the cheapest one we can find. Will the results of that behavior meet our needs over time as a firm?

Three weeks after hiring a receptionist, a senior vice president from one of our biggest client firms called me on the phone.

"Hyrum, you have a really interesting receptionist."

"Really?"

"Yeah. She doesn't speak proper English."

"She doesn't?"

"No. I called in to ask for some things and she said, 'We ain't got none o' them, Jack.'"

We learned something that day. Who is our window to the corporate world if not our receptionist? We were by then managing our firm with the Reality Model. We sat down and asked ourselves, "What principle on our corporate Belief Window allowed us to hire somebody like that?" We came up with the answer pretty fast: "Cut costs, no matter what." We decided we didn't like that principle, so we took it off our Belief Window, and we put a new one on.

The new principle we put on our Belief Window was this: "We want the finest reputation in America." A new principle on a Belief Window requires a new set of rules. We clearly needed a new receptionist, so what kind of receptionist were we going to hire now? The highest paid, finest receptionist in the state.

This was a very interesting experience for me. The person we selected to be our new receptionist was already at a director level in our firm, which had about 400 employees at the time. I called her into my office. I was excited.

"There's a new role we want you to play here at the firm. We want you to be our receptionist."

Her answer? "Why don't you just fire me, Hyrum?"

What was on her Belief Window about receptionists? She thought they were all airheads. We had to get a new principle on her Belief Window. We walked her through the whole process on how we had arrived at choosing her as our new receptionist. We gave her a raise. She got a new principle on her Belief Window. She took the job, and she became responsible for eighteen other people in our new external communications department. And this all started by putting a new principle on our corporate Belief Window.

As you experiment with the model, you will find a variety of beliefs that produce behaviors that will not meet your needs over time. (Some of them, incredibly, don't even meet your needs in the short term. You would think we would be smarter than that.) In chapter 3, I will illustrate how even young people can learn this model quickly.

CHAPTER 3

||||||||||||||||||||||||||||||||||||||||||||||||||||||||||||||||||||||||||||||||||||||||

TEACHING THE REALITY MODEL

Just like your body and lifestyle can be healthy or un-
healthy, the same is true with your beliefs. Your beliefs
can be your medicine or your poison.

—STEVE MARABOLI, *UNAPOLOGETICALLY YOU*

I would like to share with you an eye-opening experience that will help you understand how powerful the Reality Model can be. One day I was sitting in my office, which in those days was rare; the phone rang, and it was the US attorney for the district of Utah—which happens to be the entire state of Utah.

"Hyrum," he said, "I am sick and tired of locking kids up in this state for drug and alcohol abuse. I've decided to go to every high school in the state. We are going to put on a big assembly. The Utah Jazz basketball team is willing to send a player with us, and we're going to talk these kids out of drugs and alcohol. Would you go with us and do a thirty- to forty-minute talk to teach these kids how to get control of their lives?"

I got pretty excited about that. "Let's go for it," I said.

We went to 148 schools in Utah and twenty schools outside the state.

What happened at one school is particularly worth noting. On this particular day, the US attorney was not able to go; he had to be in Washington for some reason, so he sent one of his assistant attorneys, a man named Sam. The Utah Jazz basketball team was on a road trip somewhere, and could not send one of its players, so it was just Sam and me.

The school's principal met us in the lobby, took us into his office, sat us down and said, "You guys are accustomed to talking to the whole student body, right?"

I said, "Yes, we usually talk to the whole student body."

"I don't want you to talk to the whole student body, they're not the ones with the problem. I want you to talk to my druggies and alcoholics."

"Do you know who they are?"

"Of course I know who they are."

"Hey, we'll talk to anybody you want."

"Great."

He took us down to the band room, which had a stepped floor and only one door. Sam and I sat down and waited for the bell to ring. When it did, through that door came fifty of the hardest looking kids I have ever seen. I've talked to over 400,000 kids; I know what a hard kid looks like. Many of the boys had hair hanging below their shoulders. Several of them had earrings in places on their faces you would not believe; they had tattoos and studded belts with chains hanging off them.

They came in and draped themselves across the chairs in the band room, and as they looked around, they recognized each other. The hostility in the room went nuts.

The bell rang again, and the principal walked to the front of the room. Before he could open his mouth, one kid jumped out of his chair and accosted the principal: "Hey, how come we're in here anyway?"

The principal said, "Because you're all druggies and alcoholics, and these two guys are going to fix it." He then turned and walked out. I've had many introductions in my career, but this was the most interesting.

While the principal had been talking, I'd been looking at this kid and had picked him out as the ringleader of the group. He had long hair, five piercings in his face, and a big studded decorative chain hanging off his arm.

Sam was assigned to talk first. Now Sam is a wonderful guy. Putting people in jail is what he does for a living, and he's very good at it. Talking to young people is really not his thing, and this became evident really fast. Sam got up and took three steps to the front of the room. It was clear that he felt like he needed to look more like those kids, so he took off his jacket, removed his tie and threw both on a chair in the front row. Then he turned to the kids and said, "I'll tell you what, guys, if I catch you dealing drugs, I will lock you up and throw the key away. Have you got that? I will lock you up!"

The kid who had accosted the principal jumped out of his chair a second time. "The heck you will, Jack." (He didn't say "heck." Throughout the meeting I heard a very colorful vocabulary.)

"We're minors. We're under eighteen, and you can't touch us."

Then the entire group joined in, saying things like, "That's right, baby, you can't touch us."

They were right. And Sam was done. He walked back and sat down. He was supposed to talk for fifteen minutes, but he'd talked for ninety seconds. He sat next to me, leaned over and said, "You can have this mob." Sam was still for the rest of the session.

I got up and walked to the front of the room, saying to myself, You know, Hyrum, there is no way this can get any worse. But it got worse.

From the front of the room, I could see a kid about half-way back. He was disheveled and his shirt was open to his navel. He was stretched across two chairs and had tattoos everywhere. He was wearing funky glasses. And he looked to be feeling no pain whatsoever. For some reason I took him on.

I said, "Well, it looks like we have our class clown here."

He jumped out of his chair and took his glasses off. "I don't have to take that," he said.

"That's right, you don't," I shot back. "Why don't you get out?"

"Okay, I will!" He stormed toward the door, then turned around and swore at me, using three words I had never heard before. After he'd slammed the door, the entire group piped up, almost in unison: "Hey man, let's get the guy with the suit!" That's how it started.

Normally when we'd go to a high school we'd have fifteen hundred kids in a big auditorium. We'd show a film on kids who got messed up on drugs in Salt Lake City. Then one of the Utah Jazz players would get up and talk about drugs in athletics, and then the US attorney would talk, and then I'd get up and do a thirty- to forty-minute thing on how to gain control of your life. And I would teach them a poem by William Shakespeare.

But I this time I said to myself, Hyrum, if you try and teach these kids a Shakespeare poem, today is your last day on the planet. You had better do something else.

In the past I had never tried to teach the Reality Model to a group of young people, and certainly not this kind of young people. But I found myself up there, thinking, You know what? These kids are going to learn that model if it kills me. And I wasn't sure it wouldn't at that point.

So I said, "All right, listen up. I came down here to teach you a model. It's called the Reality Model. You're going to burn it into your brains before you walk out that door. I don't have a blackboard up here, so I need five volunteers. I'll pick the volunteers. You, get down here." I dragged a longhaired kid up, sat him in a chair.

"You're my Needs wheel. There are four Human Needs. Commit them to memory: to live; to love and be loved; to feel important; and to have variety. Give me one back." At first he wouldn't give me one back, but finally I got him to mutter one.

Then I picked the kid who'd been accosting everybody to be my Belief Window. It took me six minutes before I finally got his real name. He gave me eleven wrong names first. His real name was JD. I brought him up front and said, "You're my Belief Window." I finally had five kids up there, all representing a piece of the model.

"Okay, I'm going to give you a principle you might have on your Belief Window. You give me the need driving that, and let's take it through the model. Here's the principle: My self-worth is dependent on being okay with my friends."

Do you know any young people who have that principle on their Belief Window? Do you know any old people who have that principle on their Belief Window?

"Give me the need driving that," I said next.

An answer popped up: "To feel important."

I said, "Yeah, probably that. How about to be loved? Let's take that through the model. If that's what you believe, then you set up your rules. You go to a party. Some of your friends offer you drugs and alcohol, what are you going to do?"

The whole group chimed in: "We're going to take them."

"That's right, you're going to take them. Will the results of that behavior meet your needs over time?"

They didn't have the foggiest idea what I was talking about.

Identifying Correct Principles

Next we started driving stuff through the model. Twenty-five minutes into the session, JD, the kid who was my Belief Window, figured out the model.

"Okay, Hyrum." When JD jumped out of his chair, the group went stone quiet. You could see in their faces that they thought, Holy #&*%! JD is going to get the guy with the suit!

Then JD said, "Let me tell you how stupid this model is. You just told us if the results of our behavior don't meet our needs, there's an incorrect principle on our Belief Window, right?"

I was excited. He used the words perfectly. "Right," I answered. I knew exactly where he was going, so I stopped him. "Wait a minute, JD, do you drink?"

"Yeah, I drink."

"How much do you drink?"

"Eight or ten beers a week. I get wasted on weekends."

"You get wasted *every* weekend?"

"Yeah."

"Are you an alcoholic?"

"No way! You can't be an alcoholic drinking like that."

"You just gave me a principle on your Belief Window."

"I did?"

"Yeah, you did. You just told me you believe you can take eight beers a week, get wasted on weekends, and not be an alcoholic. You told me you believe that."

"So?"

"That's all, JD, just want to make sure you understand. Go ahead."

JD continued. "Okay, Hyrum, that means if the results of our behavior *do* meet our needs, there's a *correct* principle on our Belief Window, right?"

"Right."

"Okay, I have a principle on my Belief Window."

I was excited. He was using the model perfectly.

"I don't care what those kids think about me," JD continued. "The principle on my Belief Window is that drugs and alcohol are fun. And the need driving that? Variety! Take that through your stupid model. If that's true, then I set up my rules. I go to a party and my friends offer me drugs and alcohol, so I take them. Do the results of that meet my needs? You bet they do, man. When I take drugs and alcohol, I feel terrific. That means I've got a correct principle on my Belief Window, right?"

You could hear a pin drop. I stood there for a second, then answered, "Right."

And he said, "Right?"

And I said, "Yeah, right. But you forgot the second law, JD. *Results take time to measure.* You don't know yet. You may feel good that night, or over the weekend, but over time, is that going to meet your needs?"

He came back with lightning speed, "Okay, okay, man, that means I take drugs and alcohol all my life and prove it, right?"

Pretty smart kid. I said, "Yeah, you can do that. That's the dumbest way to find out if you've got a good principle on your Belief Window, but you can do that if you want."

"How else are you going to do it?"

I said, "It's called seeds and fruits."

"What does that mean?"

"That means you take a look at somebody else's life that took drugs and alcohol all their lives and see if it really met their needs. Can we do that?"

"Yeah."

I said, "Okay, JD, you give me one example." At this point we were nose to nose at the front of the room. I was dripping wet with sweat, but no one knew. I kept my coat on. "You give me one example of somebody who took drugs and alcohol all their lives where it really met their needs. One example."

Do you know what example he gave me? Elvis Presley.

"Elvis Presley?" I said. "Where's Presley, for crying out loud?"

"Dead."

"How come?"

"OD'd on drugs."

"Did that meet his needs?"

JD sat down, and I turned to the group. "Give me another example."

The second example they threw at me was Janis Joplin.

"Where's Janis Joplin?"

"Dead."

"How come?"

"OD'd on drugs."

"Did that meet her needs?"

The third example—and I am not kidding—was John Belushi.

"Where's Belushi?"

"Dead."

"How come?"

"OD'd on drugs."

"Did that meet his needs?"

For the first time, I had their undivided attention. The room was completely silent.

"Now, listen, folks. I did not come down here to tell you what belongs on your Belief Window. That is none of my business. I came down here to tell you that you've *got* a Belief Window. You've got the same four needs I've got. And you're putting principles and beliefs on that window every day that you think are going to meet your needs. Are you mature enough to take that window off, put it on the table and find out if those principles are correct?"

There was a kid with green hair that jumped out of his chair at this point and said, "This is a bunch of garbage!"

"What do you mean, this is a bunch of garbage?"

"Who cares about this stupid model? We're all going to be dead in ten years anyway."

"What do you mean, you're going to be dead in ten years?"

"Yeah, we're going to blow ourselves up."

"You just gave me a principle on your Belief Window."

"I did?"

"Yeah, you did. You just told me that you believe you'll be dead in ten years. How many of you believe that?"

Forty-three hands went up. I said, "Let's take that one through the model: We will be dead in ten years. If you believe that, and it's now time for you to perform in school, how are you going to perform in school?"

The kid sitting next to the green-haired one jumped out of his chair and said, "This is the dumbest kid in school, man, he's flunking out."

I said, "Flunking out. Are the results of that going to meet your needs over time? Suppose you're not dead in ten years. Twelve years from today, you're still alive. Who's going to buy the green dye for your hair, for crying out loud?"

I wish I had a picture of this kid. It looked like he had been hit by a baseball bat.

He stood there and said, "That doesn't mean you don't try."

"The heck it doesn't. How are you doing in school? Right now, how are you doing in school?"

The kid sitting next to him jumped up again. "This is the village idiot, man. He's flunking out."

I said, "You got many friends like him?"

The bell rang, and the door opened and the principal came back: "Your time's up."

I said, "Well, I guess our time's up."

Two kids jumped up: "No way, man, we're not done."

"We're not done? Do you want some more?" I asked.

"We've got to have another hour."

"Can't have another hour, its lunchtime," the principal announced.

"Well, can we come back after lunch?" I asked.

"I guess you can," said the principal. "Be back in your seats at 12:15."

Behavior Patterns Identify Results

At five minutes past twelve, sixty kids came into the room; that's ten more than the first group, and these ten were even harder looking. The five kids that I had up front were back in their chairs before anyone else arrived. They wanted those chairs. When they all got settled, a lot of the hostility was gone, but we weren't friends yet. I decided that I was going to try something anyway.

I needed to bring the ten new kids up to speed. "Okay guys, remember how I said that when you witness a pattern of behavior, you can tell what's on the Belief Window? Pretty much, yes, you can. Scarier than that, if you know what's on someone's Belief Window, what can you predict with great accuracy? You can predict their behavior and ultimately their results, right?"

"Yeah, that's right."

"I'm witnessing a pattern of behavior today."

They all looked at me. "What are you talking about?"

"You people look awful."

The anger and hostility returned pretty fast.

I said, "Look at you people. If you tried to run in the world I run in, you wouldn't last thirty seconds. You look horrible." Then I picked a kid out: "You, stand up." He had the most beautiful long hair I had ever seen, down below his shoulders.

"You're wearing long hair."

"So?"

"How long have you been wearing long hair?"

"Five years."

"That makes that a pattern of behavior, right?"

"Yeah."

"Well I want to know what's on your Belief Window driving you to wear long hair."

Unmet Needs Drive Behavior

The long-haired kid stood there for a full minute. Do you have any idea how long a minute is when the room is totally silent? At the end of the minute, he said, "It gets my father's attention."

Which of the four Human Needs was not being met? The need to love and be loved.

Understand that when any of these needs are not being met, all of our energy flows to meet that need, automatically. And we start putting principles on our Belief Window with lightning speed that we think will meet that need. If we put a principle on our Belief Window that drives behavior that works in the short term and destroys in the long term, will we still do it? Tragically, most of us will, unless we learn to meet our needs over time.

I wanted to win these kids back because they were all madder than heck at me. "Listen, guys," I said. "When I walked in here today, you saw a pattern of my behavior, did you not?"

"What are you talking about, man?"

"Didn't I throw a long-haired kid out of here?"

"Yeah, you did."

"Well, maybe I have something on my Belief Window."

A kid jumped up: "You think all long-haired kids are rotten."

"Well, I don't think I believe that, but let's say I do. Let's put that on my window: All long-haired kids are rotten. If that's true then, I come to your school and a long-haired kid gives me a hard time, what am I going to do?"

The whole group roared. "You're going to throw him out!"

"Right, I threw him out. Will the results of my behavior meet my needs over time?" Sixty heads in the room nodded up and down.

I said, "No, no, no. Is that kid here?"

"No."

"Is he getting the benefit of this group?"

"No."

"Will he ever speak to me again?"

"No."

"Is that meeting my needs?"

"No!"

Another kid chimed in. "You got a screwed-up Belief Window, Hyrum!"

They were starting to get it.

JD jumped out of his chair; by this time it seemed like he and I had become friends. He said, "Okay, Hyrum, there are two things we got to run through our model." He actually said "our" model. I wanted to hug him.

He continued, "First of all, why did you come down here? Why are you at our school today?"

"Because I have something on my Belief Window," I said.

"What is it?"

"Well, I have the principle on my Belief Window that I'm supposed to make a difference."

"What does that mean?"

"I don't know exactly what that means. I heard Winston Churchill give a speech before he died. The man said that he was going to make a difference. So I decided Hyrum's going to make a difference, too. Which of the four Human Needs would drive that?"

A new kid answered, "To feel important."

I said, "Yeah, and how about the need to love? Why would I come talk to a sick group like you? *Variety.* Trust me. Let's take that through the model. If that's true then, and your school asks me to come talk to you about drugs and alcohol, what am I going to do?"

The whole group answered, "You're going to do it."

Then one kid asked, "Well, Hyrum, is it meeting your needs?"

"I don't know," I answered. "Remember, it takes time to measure results. I don't know yet."

"Okay, all right, I understand that," JD said. "Now, here's the real thing." When he started talking about the real thing, he was pacing back and forth in front of the room. "There's this girl, she's my friend. She is not my girlfriend."

The minute he started talking about this girl, the group went deathly quiet. They all knew which girl he was talking about.

"She's a cocaine addict and an alcoholic. Her parents are alcoholics and cocaine addicts. They beat her all the time. They're the most screwed-up people you've ever seen. She's going to kill herself today. She called me this morning, and she said that she's taking herself out today. How are we going to keep this girl from committing suicide?"

They all expected a golden answer from the guy with the suit. I stood there for a minute and said, "I don't know."

"What do you mean, you don't know?"

"How am I supposed to know?"

"You've got a suit, you're supposed to know!"

I thought that that was an interesting belief on their Belief Window.

"Well, I *don't* know," I said. "Let's put what we know in the model. What is her behavior?"

JD answered, "I told you, she's a cocaine addict and an alcoholic."

"Will the results of her behavior meet her needs over time?" I then had the most electric teaching experience I have ever had. Sixty heads in that room shook their heads from side to side.

I said, "You've got that right. What does that mean?"

A kid stood up and said, "She's got a screwed-up Belief Window!"

JD shouted, "If I go tell her she's got a screwed-up Belief Window, she'll throw me out!"

I said, "Guys, it's deeper than a Belief Window. There's a need not being met. Which of the four needs aren't being met?"

Another kid wearing an army field jacket stood up, looking like he'd just had a revelation. Looking at me like I was a complete idiot, he said, "Nobody loves her."

I replied, "What are we going to do about that?"

The same kid, dumbfounded, looked at me and he said, "We love her, dummy."

"And how are we going to do that?"

These kids then came up with the most wonderful ideas on how they could show that girl they loved her.

"Do you think if we started showing her we loved her, we could start talking to her about principles on Belief Windows?" I asked.

"Yeah."

The bell rang again. The principal came back to tell us the time was really up. He threw everybody out, but JD lingered behind. He walked up to me and got right up in my face. "Let me tell you something. I've been in drug and alcohol therapy for ten years."

JD was at this time sixteen years old. His brother had given him cocaine when he was six.

He said, "I've been in jail four times. I've had every shrink in this state try and figure me out. This is the first time anything made any sense to me."

I stayed right there, nose to nose. "JD, I'm going to tell you this one more time. I did not come down here to tell you what belongs on your Belief Window. That is none of my business. I came down here to tell you that you've *got* a Belief Window. You've got the same needs I've got, and you're putting principles on that window every day that you think will meet your needs. Are you man enough to put that Belief Window on the table and find out what's incorrect?"

JD responded, "Yeah, I am."

"Well, I guess we'll see, won't we?"

|||||||||||||||||||||||||||||||||||||||||||||||||||||||||||||||||||||||||||||||||||||||||||

CHAPTER 4

Applying the Reality Model

If you don't change your beliefs, your life will be like this forever. Is that good news?

—ATTRIBUTED TO W. SOMERSET MAUGHAM

Now that you have read how a group of teenagers reacted to the Reality Model, I would like to complete the process of understanding the remaining five natural laws that are critical to using the model effectively.

Understanding Behavioral Responsibility

Here are two powerful facts about the Reality Model:

1. It places responsibility for behavior smack on the human being, where it belongs. I give this as my opinion: There arrives a point in our lives when we must take total responsibility for our behavior. Do you buy that?
2. You can be very confrontational when attacking somebody's Belief Window, because you're not attacking the person, you're attacking the Belief Window. You're attacking something they can fix.

Growth Requires Changing Principles

> The third natural law: Growth is the process of changing
> principles on your Belief Window.

Corporate America spends $70 billion a year training its workers. Why? Why do corporations send their people to seminars and training? To make them perform better and help them improve their behavior, right?

At a large investment firm where we trained a lot of people in time management, I shared the Reality Model with a senior training manager, and she got pretty excited about it.

"Hyrum, all the training we do here is designed to improve and enhance the behavior and productivity of our people, right?" she asked.

I said, "Right. That's probably why you do the training."

"That means that what we're really doing is trying to get new and better principles on their Belief Windows so they can govern themselves."

She was right. If you go to a class or seminar at a corporation or in public, the facilitator should say, "The principle we'd like you to have on your Belief Window as a result of this class today is—," and then lay it out. That is really the message we want people to understand.

Unmet Needs Lead to Addiction

> The fourth natural law: Addiction is the result
> of deep,and unmet needs.

Why do young people do a lot of the dumb things they do?
Why do they take drugs? Why do they act out in front of
their friends? They're trying to meet needs—powerful and
compelling needs. Why do adults do a lot of the dumb stuff
they do? Same reason. Remember, if we put principles on
our Belief Windows that drive behavior that works in the
short term and destroys in the long term, we will still do it
unless we apply the principles of the Reality Model.

The Importance of Self-Worth

> The fifth natural law: If your self-worth is dependent
> on anything external, you are in big trouble.

We get some very interesting things on our Belief Windows.
I'm going to share a couple of principles with you now, and
this time I want you to predict the behavior these principles will drive.

Here is a principle: "My self-worth is dependent on the
size of my waist." Do you know anyone who has that
principle on his or her Belief Window? What's the extreme
behavior that principle could drive? Possibly eating disor-
ders? My kids went to high school in a suburban community. Every morning at 5:30, fifty young women would
show up at the school for a rehearsal of a nationally ranked
women's drill team. They weighed every young woman

every morning; one pound overweight, and a woman was thrown off the team. They don't do that anymore, but there were nine anorexic students on that team. Do you see where this comes from?

Here's a principle a lot of men in our culture have: "My self-worth is dependent on my job, and it has to be a white-collar job." The fact that I am magnificent with my hands doesn't matter. Somewhere I've picked up that I've got to carry a briefcase like everybody else in my high school class.

Many years ago I was in Boston to lead a seminar. Sitting in the front row was an attorney. How did I know he was an attorney? He told me; he also told me *why* he was an attorney. He was the fifth generation of attorneys in his family in Boston. If you were a male baby in his home, you were destined to be an attorney.

He hated being an attorney.

Two weeks after he went through the Reality Model, he delicately approached his wife and said, "My needs are not being met by being an attorney." He was forty-nine years old, with a six-figure income. "Do you know what I want to do? I want to teach music at Boston College."

What do you think his wife said? "Have you lost your mind?"

"If I make this major career change at this point in my life, will you still love me?" he asked.

"Of course, I'll love you . . . and I'll miss you!"

This fellow made the change. He is now teaching music at Boston College. He cut his income by a factor of eight, and he is happier than he's ever been before. Is that possible? We get some really weird things on our Belief Windows about money, don't we?

By the way, his wife stayed with him.

Experiencing Inner Peace

> The sixth natural law: When the results of your behavior meet your needs over time, you experience inner peace.

The central theme of the seminar we used to teach at Franklin Quest was the acquisition and maintenance of inner peace. People were stunned to hear that in a corporate seminar. I'd be teaching a class, and about an hour into it somebody would raise his or her hand and say, "Aren't you going to teach us how to make a list?"

"Would you like to know how to make a list?"

"Well, yeah!"

"I'll teach you how to make a list, but that's not why you're here."

"It's not?"

"No."

"Why am I here?"

"You're here to get inner peace."

"Oh. Are you going to give me a planner?"

"Would you like a planner?"

"Yeah."

"I'll give you a planner, but that's not why you're here."

"It's not?"

"No."

"Why am I here?"

"You're here to get inner peace."

"Oh."

By the time we finished, they got it.

Would you like to have an eight-hour time-management seminar in nine seconds?

> Find out what matters most to you. Bring the events of your life in line with what matters most to you, and then you will have the right to inner peace.

That's all we taught. This is a six-thousand-year-old idea. It's really true, by the way. That's how inner peace comes. By the way, you owe me $295 for that eight-hour seminar.

Harmonizing the Mind

> The seventh natural law: The mind naturally seeks harmony when presented with two opposing principles.

Psychologists call the lack of harmony cognitive dissonance. We tend to resolve that by going to the principle that's going to work. Let's go back to the marriage example. We presented two principles: "Men are better than women," and "Men and women are equal." Which one will I likely pick? I'm going to pick the one that's going to work. But suppose I choose not to change that principle on my Belief Window and I stick to "Men are better than women." I show up at work tomorrow and my new boss is a woman. Do I have a problem? Has she got a problem? (If so, she can solve her problem with me pretty quickly.)

> Understand that this entire model is nothing more
> than a visual representation of what's going
> on anyway. Its power is in its simplicity.

There's not a person in the world who doesn't have those four Human Needs. You've got them. You've got Belief Windows, and they are covered with principles. Some are driving results that will meet your needs over time and, frankly, some may not be. You've got rules all set up that are driving your behavior based on what you believe to be true. Where it breaks down is that we tend not to measure the results. So there's pain, and we're not sure why.

North Philadelphia is one of the most dangerous communities in America. There are killings almost every night. We at Franklin Quest adopted a high school in the middle of North Philadelphia, the Ben Franklin High School. Years ago the principal, an amazing man named Dr. Norman Spencer, invited me to come speak to the juniors and seniors at the school. They would not allow me to drive myself into the neighborhood; it was that dangerous. Taxicabs didn't go into that neighborhood, so I was escorted in by two police squad cars. I watched them lock the doors on the inside of a four-story high school with chains at 8:30 in the morning.

I asked Dr. Spencer, "Why are you locking your doors with chains?"

"Well, that's the only way we can keep the drug pushers out of the high school."

"Oh."

Then we went into the auditorium. There were nine hundred black kids. I was the only white person within about thirty-two square blocks. If you want a sobering experience, fly to Philadelphia, rent a car, and drive into North Philadelphia. You will think you've driven into Berlin two days after the Second World War ended. It's that bleak.

I spent ninety minutes with those kids. I taught them the Reality Model. I had the Belief Window projected on a big screen. About an hour into it, I walked out into the auditorium and confronted a kid sitting on the aisle. As I walked up to him, he stood up to confront me. I got right up in his face and said, "Suppose you lived in a neighborhood where on the neighborhood Belief Window was the principle, "All blacks are stupid."

It got really quiet. This kid stood there and said, "All blacks aren't stupid."

"I didn't say they were. I said suppose you lived in a neighborhood where on the neighborhood Belief Window was the principle, "All blacks are stupid."

"All blacks aren't stupid!"

It took me four times. When he finally realized what I was doing, he looked at me and he said, "I live in a neighborhood like that."

"How much fun is that?"

"It's no fun."

From this experience we see how an engrained and seemingly simple belief can have huge consequences for an individual, a family, a city, and a culture. The results of this belief are shown through what the individuals, families, and culture do. Sometimes the beliefs are helpful, and sometimes they are hurtful.

Prejudgments and Prejudices

All of our prejudgments or prejudices are principles on Belief Windows, are they not? All blacks are. . . . All Hispanics are. . . . All rich people are. . . . All poor people are. . . . And so on. Those principles can drive some very painful behavior, can they not? If that behavior is ever going to change, what has to change first? The principle on the Belief Window has to change first or the behavior will never change. Maybe all blacks aren't, maybe all Hispanics aren't, and so on.

I grew up in Honolulu, and I spent my first eighteen years in Hawaii. It never occurred to me to be prejudiced. I was one of five white kids in a class of sixty nonwhite kids. I had to come to Los Angeles to discover that prejudice is alive and well in the United States.

You have learned the Reality Model and the seven natural laws that make it work. In order to make changes in a Belief Window that is causing negative results, it is necessary to learn how to use the model.

|||||||||||||||||||||||||||||||||||||||||||||||||||||||||||||||||||||||||||||||||||||||

USING THE REALITY MODEL

Whenever we seek to avoid the responsibility for our own behavior, we do so by attempting to give that responsibility to some other individual or organization or entity. But this means we then give away our power to that entity.

—M. SCOTT PECK, *THE ROAD LESS TRAVELED*

In chapter 4 we learned the power of the Reality Model by hearing how it was taught to high school kids who were addicted to drugs and alcohol. The model can be used by anyone in life, under any life circumstance. It doesn't simply fix things; it can also improve things that are already quite good. The goal of this chapter is for you to learn in depth the steps involved in using the model in your own life and to be able to teach it to someone else.

Five Steps

Let me introduce you to five steps on how to use this model in a very simple but powerful way. Each step begins with the letter "A" to help you remember them more easily.

Step 1: ADMIT That There Are Areas of Pain in Your Life

One of the greatest obstacles to changing our lives for the better is the refusal to admit that we need to change. If you don't admit you are overweight, you are not likely to take steps to lose weight. If you don't admit that your marriage is in trouble, you will never take the difficult steps to fix it. If you don't admit that your work performance is not meeting your organization's needs, you will not try to improve it. The fact is that all of us could probably sit down and list at least half a dozen areas of our lives where our results are not fully meeting our needs. (And it wouldn't take long to do it.) The two reasons we don't do that are (1) we may not realize that we can do anything about it, and (2) it is painful to do.

Step 2: ACCEPT That the Person at Fault for the Pain Is the One Staring Back at You in the Mirror

Almost all of us succumb to the temptation to "externalize" our problems. We look for someone or something else to blame when we are in pain, when we fail to meet our goals, or when our relationships hit rocky ground. The fact is that although external circumstances are often part of the problem, we can do little or nothing about changing them, so we should be happy to admit that we are the ones to blame for these problems, at least in ways we can affect or change. If it truly was the doing of someone else, there would not be much we could do about it. The fact that these issues lie within our power to change is the most uplifting message we can hear. It means that there is hope for improvement.

Step 3: ASK Two Critical Questions

The first question you must ask yourself is <u>what</u> behaviors of yours are leading to the pain or shortfall in your life. Remember the Reality Model: behavior leads directly to results. For most of us, when weight is the problem, our behaviors around eating and/or exercising usually are key drivers of the problem. It may not be as easy to identify the behaviors driving other areas of pain. If you have trouble figuring it out, you can always ask your spouse, partner, or best friend. I promise you, it won't take long to get the answer. Remember, behavior is the only truly visible piece of the model. That is where we have to start.

For about four years, every six months, I'd visit a place in Utah called the Point of the Mountain. It is the location of the Utah State Penitentiary.

The first time I was there, I was given ninety inmates in blue uniforms. We were in a cafeteria in the basement of this big prison, and I had my Reality Model up on the blackboard. We were about ninety minutes into it, and I said, "Okay, guys. You exhibited some behavior that got you into this place, right?"

"Yeah, that's right."

"Is that behavior going to meet your needs over time? Do you guys want to talk about time?" They did *not* want to talk about time. "If you people get out of here, what's the probability of your coming back?" I asked.

"Oh, we all come back."

"Right. You all come back, which means what didn't change?"

"Our behavior."

"Of course—your behavior didn't change. You're back in jail. Let's go deeper than that. What else didn't change?"

"Our Belief Window."

I said, "If you want to get out of here and stay out, what do you have to do surgery on while you're here?"

"We've got to change our Belief Window."

A craggy-faced inmate came up to me at the end, tears streaming down his face. He shook my hand, looked me in the eye, and said, "Hyrum, you've given me the key to how I'm going to get out of here tonight." I wasn't sure how to take that, but he was excited.

This illustrates the second question that you must ask yourself and answer. That question is _why_. Once you know the behavior that is causing the painful results, you need to identify possible principles on your Belief Window that lead to that behavior. I use the word "possible" because you are not going to become a psychologist when you finish this book. How do you do this? You start asking the question _why_. Why the behavior? Why are you wearing long hair? Why are you smoking pot? Think about the answer, and remember this:

> The answer to the question *why* always surfaces in the form of a principle on a Belief Window. Always.

The following examples show how a problem causing pain can be connected to a behavior pattern and from there to an underlying belief that makes the behavior seem rational.

Area of pain: My boss is mad at me. I think he may demote me.

Behavior: I am late to every meeting the boss calls.

Belief: I am important enough that they won't start the meeting without me.

Area of pain: My daughter is always mad at me and never talks to me.

Behavior: I yell at her a lot, trying to get her to do things the way I want.

Belief: Good parents make sure their kids don't make any mistakes.

Area of pain: I am forty pounds overweight and my joints hurt all the time.

Behavior: I eat a lot of fast foods and desserts, and snack late at night.

Belief: I have a great metabolism that should take care of what I eat.

You get the idea. These examples of beliefs may be simplistic (or they may strike a chord), but they serve to illustrate the importance of finding the belief that is driving the behavior. Remember, your rules are automatic. Unless the belief changes, the behavior will not change.

By the way, this model is a wonderful way to study history. Years before we got into the Second World War, did we know what Adolf Hitler had on his Belief Window? We knew. How did we know? He wrote a book; he told us.

Could we have predicted his behavior knowing that? A lot of people did predict it. It's just that it was so ugly that no one would believe it for about six years.

One of the principles on Hitler's Belief Window was that the races are graded. There are higher races and lower races. What was the highest race for Adolf Hitler? Aryans. The lowest races were Jews and Blacks. Could we predict his behavior knowing he believed that?

Did the results of his behavior meet his needs over time? How long did the Thousand-Year Reich last? Twelve years. Fifty million lives were lost because of one messed-up Belief Window.

Do we know what Osama bin Laden had on his Belief Window? We know. How do we know? He wrote about it as a teenager. Do you know who he believed he was? He believed he was the reincarnation of Saladin, who in the twelfth century broke the back of the Crusades. Saladin was probably one of the best field commanders in military history, and that is who bin Laden believed he was. Take that through the model. If that's true, then what is it bin Laden had to do? He had to kill the infidels. Where are the infidels? Wherever "nonbelievers" are.

Do you know who Saddam Hussein believed he was? He believed he was the reincarnation of Nebuchadnezzar, the Persian king who killed thousands of people and conquered what was then the known world. That's who Saddam Hussein thought he was.

Do we know what John Adams, Benjamin Franklin, Thomas Jefferson, and George Washington had on their Belief Windows? We know. How do we know? They wrote

them down. We have their letters and writings, and ultimately the Constitution of the United States.

Do we know what Dr. Martin Luther King Jr. believed?
We do. He wrote about it from the Birmingham Jail in
1963. Do we know what Mother Teresa had on her Belief
Window? We do. In addition to the patterns of behavior
that demonstrated what she believed, she wrote it all down
in a book in 2009.

Step 4: ADOPT a New Belief That Will Better Meet Your Needs over Time

You may need to spend some time thinking about this. And
it may feel awkward at first. After all, there is a reason the
old principle was on your Belief Window: you believed it
was true. If you have spent your life believing all Doberman
pinschers are vicious, and have reacted accordingly, imprinting a new belief that most Dobermans are friendly
will take some time.

Once they get the basic model, young people pick up on
this step with lightning speed. Franklin Quest adopted
another school in Salt Lake City, the Redwood Elemen-
tary School. It's a school for at-risk children. Half the students show up without shoes and coats in the winter;
many of them only have one parent living at home. It's in a
pretty tough area. Our colleagues at Franklin spend a lot
of time there.

Once I went there to speak to the fifth and sixth grad-
ers. These kids were little, ten or eleven years old; there were
150 of them sitting on the floor of the cafeteria. I spoke to
them for ninety minutes; I made them take notes. I came

back to my office and thought, Man, those kids hate me. I'll never be asked back. Did they even understand what I was talking about?

Three weeks later I was in a service station, midway between my office and their school. I was putting gas in my car when, out of nowhere, a little kid came around the back of the car and said, "Hey, is that going to meet your needs over time?"

He got it!

If you have teenagers in your home, teach them the model. You will discover that you now have a way of talking to that teenager in a way that you're not attacking them. You're sitting side by side looking at their Belief Window.

"I'm okay, Dad—right?"

"I love you a lot, kid, but you've got a screwed-up Belief Window, and we are going to do surgery on it."

Step 5: ACT as If the New Principle Were True

In the last several decades, neuroscience has found that our brains are constantly developing and rewiring themselves based on what we learn and what we experience. Imprinting a new principle on a Belief Window is the same as developing a new habit. At first, it will seem awkward, and you will have to consciously remind yourself that you believe in a new way. Over time, especially as you see the results of the new behaviors that grow out of your new principle, it will become a natural part of you.

The simplest way to implement the *act as if* principle is to repeat it, verbally or mentally, every time you're resistant to trying a new behavior. These are known as affirmations, and they represent the mental rewiring of the mind/window as a critical first step to the physical behavior that solidifies that rewiring process.

I don't mean to make this sound like it is easy, or like it is a steady, gradual climb to a new reality. In fact, there are going to be ups and downs. You will slip back into old patterns, but the key is to avoid getting upset with yourself when that happens. Just as the two-year-old falls when learning to walk, you will stumble a bit as you adopt a new principle on your Belief Window. Stick with it, and you will take some pain out of your life.

Failure Is Part of Growth

When my son was in high school, he got onto the basketball team. He developed a peculiar behavior. Every time he'd shoot a ball in a game and miss, he'd stop shooting for the rest of the game. If he ran into one of the opposing players, he'd back off and stop being aggressive. If he received a bad grade in school, he would implode; he would get really ugly when he got bad grades. This was his behavior.

My son understands the Reality Model. Why? I've burned it into his brain, and he has it tattooed to his right thigh. (That's a joke.) Now, remember, I'm not going to attack my son. What am I going to attack? Something he can fix: his Belief Window.

One Sunday morning I sat down with my son. We were both still in our pajamas.

I said, "Joseph, can I share some behavior that I've been observing? (This is the first question mentioned above: the *what*.) Then I asked him if we could identify some possible principles that might be driving that behavior. (This is the second question: the *why*.)

He responded, "Sure, Dad. What's the problem?"

"Well, son, here's your behavior. Every time you shoot a ball in a game and miss, you stop shooting for the rest of the game. You've got the best shot on the team, but you stop shooting. When you run into one of the other players, you back off and stop being aggressive. When you get a bad grade in school you get really ugly."

I then moved into the drill-down process and started asking the question *why*. "Why do you back off? Why do you stop shooting? Why do you get so ugly when you get bad grades?"

This didn't happen quickly. Remember, the answer always comes up in the form of a principle on a Belief Window. There were all kinds of weird principles on that kid's Belief Window. But your gut tells you when you get to the big one, the bedrock.

Twenty-five minutes into this conversation, my son sat there in a very reflective mood. He looked at me, then said, "Well, Dad, I think you need to understand that I am really afraid of failing."

A big red flag went up in my brain.

"Joseph, I think we've found the principle on your Belief Window, and the principle is *failure is bad*. Where did you get a principle like that?" My son looked up at me. He didn't have to say anything.

Where did he get it? From me, his dad. He immediately became emotional. "Come on, Dad. You don't know anything about failure."

"What do you mean I don't know anything about failure?"

He was shaking. "You can't even *spell* failure, Dad. You go all over the world giving speeches. Everybody thinks you're terrific. You've got your own private plane, for crying out loud! You don't know anything about failure."

I said, "Listen, kid, let me tell you about my failures."

I then spent over an hour detailing my personal failures. Five major financial disasters. I made the mistake of telling him about my grades in school. I recommend you don't do that, by the way, but I did.

When I finished, Joseph looked at me and said, "You mean it's okay to fail, Dad?"

"Yeah, it's okay, son. All you have to do is fix it after you've messed up.

We put a new principle on his Belief Window that day about failure. And the new principle is, "Failure is a part of growth." Two days later I watched him play in another basketball game. He started shooting when he shouldn't shoot. He was lobbing forty-footers. He started to enjoy hurting the other team.

The coach had to pull him out of the game. "You're going to hurt somebody, kid. You're an animal. Now, sit down."

He came home one day with a D on an exam, triumphant. "I got a D, Dad. Have you ever seen one of those?" (I had.)

We had to have a whole new conversation about grades and Belief Windows. But the minute he placed a new principle on his Belief Window about failure, a lot of pain went out of his life.

Teaching the model to those we know and love can drastically change the trajectory of their lives. When a Belief Window is changed to "Failure is okay as long as you fix it," then tremendous growth and learning can begin. Why? Because we learn to identify why we are getting the results we get—by becoming aware of principles on our Belief Windows.

||||||||||||||||||||||||||||||||||||||||||||||||||||||||||||||||||||||||||||||||||||||||||||||||||||||

CHAPTER 6

ORGANIZATIONAL APPLICATION

Culture is the deeper level of basic assumptions and
beliefs that are shared by members of an organization.

—EDGAR SCHEIN, *ORGANIZATIONAL CULTURE AND LEADERSHIP*

The preceding chapters have focused on you as an individual. We have talked about your Belief Window and whether you are meeting your needs over time. But each one of us is more than just an individual. We are members of a number of organizations, from families to corporations. Whether you are an employee striving to make a meaningful contribution, an executive trying to steer the ship, or the head of a family, this chapter is for you.

Meeting Our Needs over Time

I don't think anyone sets out to "meet payroll" or to build an organization like we did at Franklin Quest, where literally thousands of families rely on the decisions you make every day. But we did build that organization, and we did assume the responsibility—in partnership with everyone we worked with—to serve our customers, to meet payroll, and to make a difference in people's lives.

And, when you do that, you jump into the deep end of the pool: everything the Reality Model is about. There were many times in the building of this global company that I consciously asked myself, Will this decision meet our needs over time?

And I do know that that question matters as much in the boardroom and the executive suite as it does anywhere else. And maybe it even matters more there, because so many people rely on the answer and because we're dealing with real life, real consequences, and real outcomes that have real and lasting impacts on people, their lives, and their relationships.

This part of the book is about being a leader, holding leadership responsibility, and trying to do the right thing day in and day out. And in knowing that the right thing shares, at least in part, the very real question and the answers it drives: Will this meet our needs over time?

This is about applying what we've learned about the Reality Model in the preceding chapters to our managerial and leadership responsibilities. As a leader, I've learned that the Reality Model and the principles it's based upon are always at play—at home and at work. This chapter is about the "at work" part.

Leadership and the Human Needs Pyramid

A dictionary definition of the word *organization* might be a "group of persons and things dedicated to a specific goal." In other words, organizations are nothing more than groups of individuals taking things (resources) and focusing them, and their energies, on outcomes that will hopefully meet their needs now and over time.

Since organizations are made up of individuals, it makes sense to me that the needs that drive one person are probably very similar to—if not exactly the same as—the needs that drive an organization.

Let's reexamine the four Human Needs in an organizational context.

The Need to Live (Physiological Need)

People need food, shelter, water, safety, security, and all of the other things that Abraham Maslow and others have mentioned. I'm going to use Maslow's hierarchy of needs, first expressed in in his 1943 essay "A Theory of Human Motivation," to frame the Reality Model and an organization's needs.

Organizations, like individuals, need to sustain life. Organizations don't eat chicken, mashed potatoes, and peas. What they eat is money, markets, inventory, and all of the other materials that allow them to find, serve, and retain their customers. If you don't think organizations, like people, have to eat to live, you've never seen the changes that occur between the top and bottom lines of an income statement or a balance sheet. Organizations are hungry, and it's a leader's job to feed that hunger yet to keep the organization lean (though not too lean), to give it the energy it needs to get through the day, the month, and the years to come.

The Need to Love and Be Loved (Belonging)

If you want to guarantee a phone call from your Human Resources department, as a leader of an organization go out and teach everyone that we, as members of the organization, need to "love and be loved." I think that, as a general rule, we ought not to take the "love and be loved" idea too far in an organization unless we're running a family business. But if we get to the real root of that statement, we're right on target for understanding how this need works in an organization. The need to love and be loved is a profound form of the need for relationships. We all need and want them.

As the great poet John Donne wrote, "No man is an island." We are in this thing together. Relationships matter. In fact, as my friend Tony Robbins has said, "The quality of your life is in direct proportion to the quality of your relationships." And since you spend so many hours of your life at work, relationships at work are vital to your emotional well-being.

If your employees and team members are enjoying healthy relationships, then that need is met and your organization is on its way to flourishing. As in Maslow's hierarchy of needs, the need to love and be loved cannot stand alone, but it provides one of the building blocks of a healthy organization.

Relationships are the foundation of the culture, and the culture in an organization is what holds the strategy and the vision and processes together. A dysfunctional culture certainly affects your strategy, your vision, your processes, *and* your bottom line.

If you're not quite sure how important relationships are to organizational success, watch an organization try to function that has operational "silos." Watch the waste created through duplication of effort and crossover when Department A is not talking to or strategizing with Department B. Watch the confusion that reigns when the strategic vision in the Northeast Region is at cross-purposes with that of the Southwest Region. If you want to see how important the relationship need is to organizational health, simply observe the consequences of its absence.

Nothing will tear an organization apart faster than toxic relationships in the boardroom or on the senior team. Fractured organizations are not accidental; they are the consequence of relationship failures at the highest levels of the organization. You don't need your senior team to "love and be loved" in a sentimental way, but they darn sure better have quality professional relationships and respect; if not, you'll see a toxicity wash through the entire organization.

If you want a healthy company with the potential to meet its needs over time, to be here next Friday and twenty years from next Friday, work on the quality of the relationships at the highest levels of leadership.

There's some argument among economists as to whether "trickle-down economics" really share the wealth in a group. I'm not an economist, but in the area of executive leadership I've got more than enough experience—both positive and negative—to know that "trickle-down relationships" can either steer the corporate ship into the safe channel or onto the rocks.

Relationships matter. An organization consists of people, but a whole person is made up of a mental dimension, a physical part, a social/emotional part, and a spiritual part. In simple terms: mind, body, heart, and spirit. It is what my friend Stephen Covey has referred to as the Whole Person Paradigm.

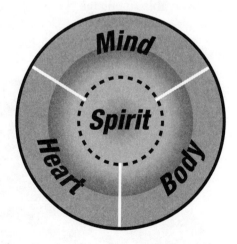

When you acknowledge the importance of relationships in an organization, you look for ways to engage the whole person: his or her mind, body, heart, and spirit. Do not doubt this fact: if a relationship is suffering, the entire output for the organization will suffer. Why? As Covey has written in his book *The 8th Habit: From Effectiveness to Greatness*, "People make choices. Consciously or subconsciously, people decide how much of themselves they will give to their work depending on how they are treated and on their opportunities to use *all* four parts of their nature. These choices range from rebelling or quitting to creative excitement."

At Franklin Covey we published the Employee Engagement Model; it recognizes the importance of relationships and the fact that employees have choices. At the lowest level, they can rebel or quit, and at that level you honestly hope that they quit. At the opposite end of the model they feel a creative excitement about their opportunities. At this level, through your healthy and positive relationship with them, you have been able to engage the whole person. Relationships do matter.

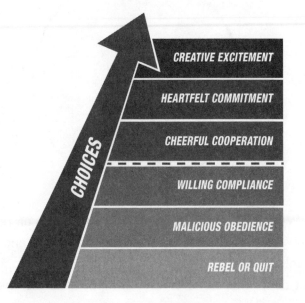

The Need to Feel Important (Esteem)

As I have traveled and taught these principles to people all over the world, I've learned that there are some elements of business culture that are far more American than we realize, and then there are elements that are universal.

For example, one of those elements of business culture is sports and its relationship with business. People everywhere love sports; in fact, the cultural and individual love for football (what we call soccer) is so profound in areas outside the United States as to be almost incomprehensible to most of us. If you think the Super Bowl is a big deal, understand this: it lasts one weekend per year. In most of the world, the World Cup lasts an entire month and the final game is watched by over 500 million people.

Accepting that a passion for sports is a global thing, it's always been interesting to me how much more we, as Americans, are ready to embed sports into business—and especially business leadership. Many American business leaders know the Vince Lombardi quote; some have it framed on their office wall: "Winning isn't everything; it's the only thing."

There's no such thing as a "Who's Lombardi?" group leading an American business. I don't know why this is. Maybe it's because, growing up, most of us experience the realities of sports before we experience the realities of business. Maybe it's because the metaphors and parallels are so obvious. All I know is, you're not likely to get through a day of business without some discussion of sports and its connection to business.

One of the great things about sports, from the little league to the professional level, is that it simplifies the complexities of life. There's a game; there are some rules; and there's the opportunity to win or lose. As much as people try nowadays to give everyone a ribbon for just showing up, we all know deep in our gut that you have either won or lost.

You didn't show up "just to have fun." You got on the field or the court or the pitcher's mound to do one thing: to win. And that's what makes business and sports such obvious companions. Business isn't about trying; it's not about "having a good time." It's about winning, because those who win make payroll; those who don't, *don't*. It's about that simple.

And it's in the pursuit of winning that we have the chance to contribute, to be a part of something bigger than ourselves, to put our talents, our brains, and our hearts on the line. It's in the pursuit of the win we can make a difference. And it's in that moment of making a difference that we feel important.

Of course, you don't have to win to feel important. But having won some and lost some, I know this much: it's a lot easier to feel important when you're on the winning side. It's a lot easier to see the genius of your idea, the value of your suggestion, the power of your creativity, when that input creates output.

I don't know of many people—unless they believe they can turn it around—who want to join a losing team. We want to win. We want to make a difference. And when we do, we feel important.

Too often organizations focus on the idea of recognizing people as the key to making those people feel important. Recognition matters, but it's a whole new ball game (there's that sports thing again) when you can recognize an idea *and* show how that idea got put to work in ways that served customers, grew revenues, created jobs, built communities, and changed the world.

Recognition opens the door; sincerity and implementation seal the deal. Creating organizational cultures that put people and ideas to work on matters of substance in ways that drive results is key. It's key to making people, teams, and entire organizations feel important. It's key to engaging the whole person.

I'm a child of what Tom Brokaw has called "the greatest generation." One of the characteristics that makes this generation great is its quiet humility. It's hard, even today, to get those that are still with us to talk about what they did. Make no mistake, they literally saved freedom. But, when these heroes talk, they don't talk about Iwo Jima or Utah Beach as an opportunity.

They talk about what they did. They talk about surviving, having a buddy's back, looking death and hell in the face, and coming out of a trench to charge forward. And they talk about winning. They didn't go to war to try; they went to war to win. And they did. And, even if they're too humble to admit it, they ought to feel important. They won. We won. Freedom won. And they're damn important—to us and to history.

As a leader, it's my job to create an environment where people can feel important, where they can feel part of something bigger than just themselves, where they can feel like they're not just being heard but that what we're hearing we're trying and doing. And they need to know that in that trying, we're changing the world.

Watch what happens to the energy in your organization when this culture of "feeling important" takes hold. Watch how the ideas multiply, the synergy swells, and the input soars.

Everyone knew that kid in second grade who constantly put her hand up because she knew she had the answer. If she found a teacher who'd keep calling on her rather than one that told her to put her hand down and let others participate, she flourished. If she felt shut down she did exactly that: she would shut down. She would realize that always having the answer was not "cool." And when she realized that having all the answers was not "cool," something very precious was lost.

Get your people raising their hands. Let them all answer. Take it all in. Sort through the answers for quality, of course, but wherever possible, put as much of it to work as you can. Because every idea that goes to work is tied to a person who offered it up in the first place. And, when people see their ideas take flight, they rise up with them. There's no better example, in leadership, of an organization "rising up on eagle's wings"—where its people and ideas are important and where ideas take flight.

The Need for Variety

Charles Dickens was a brilliant writer. He has, perhaps more than any other writer in the English language, captured the mood of his times. Substantial to both Dickens's writing and the English world of the mid- to late nineteenth century was the rise of industry—with all the blessings and curses that entailed.

When Dickens describes the workhouse, the laundry, the factory, or the orphanage of his day, he is painting a vivid picture of what it meant to live, eat, drink, sleep, and suffer the realities of low-paying, soul-grinding menial labor.

Years later, in his seminal film *Modern Times*, Charlie Chaplin turned Dickens's idea into the metaphor of the little man caught up in the industrial machine.

I'm not suggesting that the Industrial Revolution was a bad thing. (It was Marx—Karl, not Groucho—who said that.) In fact, I think that the Industrial Revolution played a major—if not the primary—role in bringing the world the standard of living many enjoy today.

But one thing factory work never brought was variety. Whether you were running fabric through a sewing machine, putting steel blanks in a stamping press, or stacking crate after crate on a loading dock, you were engaged in mundane, mind-numbing labor. And the hours were long; at the end of a day or week doing that kind of work you were left with precious little time for family, friends, or entertainment.

That life simply was not meeting the human need over time. And that's why unions were of such importance; among other things, they helped the average laborer, industrialized production, and changed the length of the workday and workweek, creating something still very rare in much of the world: leisure time.

What did we do with our leisure time? We pursued variety. The global changes in lifestyle that leisure time created can be summed up in a simple comparison to Saturday morning.

In some households, Saturday morning is an opportunity to sleep in and recover from the week's exertions. In others it's a "get up early and get the chores done so we can go to town" day. In still others, it's a chaotic chase after soccer practice, piano lessons, dance recitals, and the multitude of other activities that define so many young families and their pursuit of generational variety. Some garden, some run, some shop, some read, some work, and some play. And some just dream. But in any given town, on any given Saturday morning, what you're seeing is variety at work.

Variety makes people happy; it makes them smile. In the workplace, variety can make them smile Monday through Friday as much as it does on Saturday, which is why a business leader ought to care. Give your people variety and they'll smile more, and they'll work better; they'll be more hopeful and uplifted and feel less hopeless and downhearted.

Some jobs, of course, require repetition. We still sew shirts, make parts, and load trucks. But we're finding ways to do this in a more engaging way. In some cases we've put robots to work on the most mind-numbing tasks. In others we engage concepts like job sharing, assignment rotation, and swing shifts to make sure no one feels trapped in a job or career.

We live in a society where we get opportunities to try new things, test our talents, change jobs, move around, and pursue—not always with perfect success—a number of things we think we might enjoy. This opportunity to seek variety in career as well as in life seems so much a part of life today we can forget that it's a fairly modern phenomenon.

There are many things that typify a modern, millennial corporation. There are things that make Apple obviously Apple and not a tweaked form of IBM. And one of those things that Apple, Google, Facebook, Twitter, and so many other "top of mind" organizations share is their understanding of the importance of providing variety to their employees.

If you want to send Gen Xers or "millennials" running in the opposite direction, stick them in a cubicle, tell them to be there at exactly 8:00 a.m. and not leave one second before 5:00 p.m., and suggest that they take their Ritalin, manage their energy, and get down to the work of stacking ones and zeros like their grandparents stacked cases on the loading dock. It's no longer tolerated. The Patrick Henrys of our century cry out "Give me variety, or give me my severance, 'cause I'm outta here!"

As a leader of a twenty-first-century organization your job is simple: if you want to attract, engage, and keep talented people you better be bringing a big bowl of variety. How do you do this? You get to know those around you. You ask them questions. You take the time to discover what type of variety they need in order to be wholly and creatively engaged.

Ask those around you:

- Are there unmet needs and opportunities that we are not pursuing?

- What do you think we could do in order to make a greater contribution?
- What do you like doing?
- What opportunities exist here that you are excited about? What are we lacking?
- What capabilities do you have that could be developed and utilized?
- What do you like best about your job? What would make it better?

Management assumes that people should be grateful to have a job—period. Leadership, on the other hand, acknowledges that you want to have more than an employee's back: you want his or her heart, too; you want the whole person. But you'll never understand what employees need—what variety needs are not being met—unless you first take the time to ask.

|||||||||||||||||||||||||||||||||||||||||||||||||||||||||||||||||||||||||||||||||||||||||||||

CHAPTER 7

POWER IN THE REALITY MODEL

When we are no longer able to change a situation . . . we are challenged to change ourselves.

—VIKTOR FRANKL, *MAN'S SEARCH FOR MEANING*

In chapter 6 we saw examples of people throughout history who had different Belief Windows. The principles on those Belief Windows had some devastating results in some situations and some tremendously positive and fulfilling results in others. See if you can identify if the people in chapter 6 were pessimists, optimists, or realists.

The Pessimist, the Optimist, and the Realist

Let's take a look at three more definitions: The pessimist, the optimist, and the realist. These are Belief Window issues. Admiral James Stockdale was the highest-ranking officer in Vietnam to be taken as a prisoner of war; he spent seven and a half years in captivity. In his book *Good to Great: Why Some Companies Make the Leap . . . and Others Don't*, Jim Collins talks about the Stockdale paradox. Stockdale discovered three distinct groups in the prison in Hanoi: pessimists, optimists, and realists. He discovered the same three groups of people that Viktor Frankl discovered at Auschwitz during the Second World War. These are Stockdale's definitions:

- The pessimist sees the brutal facts and quits.
- The optimist has boundless faith and ignores the brutal facts.
- The realist sees the brutal facts and has faith they can be dealt with.

Realists Survive

The pessimists and the optimists never came home from Hanoi; they never got out of Auschwitz. They died there.

I understand why the pessimists died. They saw the brutal facts: "We're in the middle of southeast Asia, we are eight thousand miles from home, there is no way the marines are going to get in here and save us; we're toast, guys." They gave up and died. A lot of physically able people died.

The optimists surprised me. Why would the optimists die? They have boundless faith. They said, "Hey guys, we're going to be out of here by Christmas. If we're not out of here by Christmas, we'll be out of here by Valentine's Day." They ignored the brutal facts. When they weren't out by Christmas and they weren't out by Valentine's Day, what happened to the second group? They became pessimists; they died.

The realists survived. Why? They saw the brutal facts: "We're in the middle of Southeast Asia, we're eight thousand miles from home, the marines are not coming in here. Guys, we're going to be here for a long time, so let's work together to survive this." They had faith they could deal with it. Some pretty emaciated bodies survived because of that.

The question is, which are you? This is a Belief Window issue. Are we experiencing any kind of adversity right now in our country? Are there any brutal facts we have to deal with right now—in our country and globally? How about at work, or within our own families?

A Principle to Ponder

I'm going to ask you now to consider a principle for your Belief Window. I discovered this principle many years ago when I lost a daughter and granddaughter in a car accident. It was a very difficult time for my wife and me. Let me introduce the principle with this experience.

About three or four weeks after September 11, 2001, I received a call from the office of Rudy Giuliani, then the mayor of New York City. He said, "Hyrum, we've got a lot of people in pain here because of what happened on 9/11. Would you and your partner Stephen Covey come and do a full-day workshop for the families affected by 9-11?"

"Of course we will," I answered.

"The Midtown Sheraton Hotel's going to donate the ballroom and they'll donate your room, but we can't pay you."

"Fine."

We flew to New York on October 18. I've flown into New York hundreds of times, but this time was different: the Twin Towers of the World Trade Center were gone.

The next morning, the mayor arranged for a tour of Ground Zero. It was just Franklin Covey CEO Bob

Whitman, Stephen Covey, and me. A policeman picked us up at 5:00 a.m. and we drove down to the World Trade Center site. The average person could not get anywhere near Ground Zero at that point because sixteen hundred policemen cordoned it off. We went through four separate checkpoints to get there.

About a quarter past five, we were standing at Ground Zero on fifteen feet of compacted debris. We were looking at this huge hole. You can't imagine the size of that hole unless you were there. I had previously taught many seminars in the World Trade Center; I couldn't believe it was gone.

The policeman who was our escort started to tell us his story. He was very animated.

"I was here that day." He pointed. "I was standing right over there. All of a sudden I heard this big boom, and I looked up and all this stuff came flying out of the World Trade Center. It looked like paper at first, and then it started hitting the ground. It was fifty-foot I-beams, killing everybody they hit. I watched thirty-four people jump from the tower. Four of them were holding hands when they jumped. I watched eight firemen lose their lives because people fell on them."

He looked at me and asked, "Mr. Smith, how many computers do you think there were in the World Trade Center?"

"Well, a lot. Fifty thousand people worked there."

"We haven't found one computer."

"Really, how come?"

"A three-thousand-degree fire, and it is still burning."

While he was talking, a crane pulled an I-beam out of the rubble. It was dripping molten steel at the bottom even then, more than five weeks after 9/11.

The policeman continued, "You know, when that second building came down, we all thought we were dead, but I crawled under a truck and somehow I survived."

That's how our morning started.

We went back up to the Midtown Sheraton; we had to shower because we were covered with soot. We came down to the ballroom, which was designed to hold 1,800 people. There were 2,400 jammed into it. The meeting began with two policemen and two firemen in formal dress uniforms marching in with the American flag. That wiped me out. Then the Girls Choir of Harlem marched in and sang three patriotic songs. Sixty beautiful young women. They blew the roof off the place. I was a mess. I was grateful that Stephen Covey was going to speak first.

Stephen got up and did his thing. Then it was my turn. I made my way to the front of the ballroom. People were sitting on the floor. Before I could open my mouth, about halfway back in the ballroom a fireman jumped out of his chair, shouted at me and said, "Mr. Smith, are you going tell us how to get out of bed in the morning when we just don't give a crap anymore?"

That's how it started. This turned out to be one of the toughest, and yet most rewarding, speaking experiences I have ever had.

I said these words to the fireman, and this is what I want you to ponder:

> Pain is inevitable; misery is optional.

I continued, "What principle, what point am I trying to make here? The fact is, bad things happen to good people, do they not? The fact is we're not going to get through this mortal experience without some pain. How we choose to deal with that pain is ultimately dependent on what stays on our Belief Window. And by the way, the thing that separates you and me from the rest of the animal kingdom is that we can change our beliefs. We're in charge of our Belief Window."

And then I taught this group exactly what I've shared with you in this book. It was an electrifying experience.

When I finished, I said, "I will never minimize or put down what happened here on 9/11. This was bad. But just for a moment, would you compare what happened here to what's happened on this planet in the last one hundred and fifty years? What happened here on 9/11 doesn't even come up on the scope of ugliness compared to other events in that period. Does it?

"Let's go back to June sixth, 1944. No, let's go back to June fifth, 1944. Eisenhower was in a bunker in England. You know what he said to his generals? He wrote about this in his memoirs. He said, 'Gentlemen, we've got to throw more kids at that beach tomorrow than they have bullets in the bunker.' He estimated within five hundred how many he'd lose. So, you know what they did the next day? They threw two hundred thousand kids at that beach in France. Do you know what happened? The Nazis ran out of bullets in the bunker. How often do we reverence that?

"Iwo Jima was supposed to be a four-day battle in the Pacific. It lasted thirty-six days. There were eight thousand marines dead and twenty thousand wounded. There were twenty-two thousand Japanese soldiers killed. How often do we reverence that? The killing fields in Cambodia were in the millions. Stalin killed fifty million of his own people."

Some of the most serene, magnificent, amazing and wonderful people I have ever known are people who have gone through excruciating pain. But they have decided not to be miserable. And by deciding not to be miserable, they don't make other people miserable. You know what the neat thing about 9/11 was? You couldn't buy an American flag for about nine months. And it was also suddenly okay for a man to cry.

Are you an optimist, a pessimist, or a realist? We may be any of the three at various times, depending on the situation. If we begin applying the Reality Model, we should start to recognize which of the three we are, in each situation. Gaining this skill will add tremendous value to our personal lives, as well as the lives of others we come in contact with.

CHAPTER 8

||||||||||||||||||||||||||||||||||||||||||||||||||||||||||||||||||||||||||||||||||||||||||

INNER PEACE

What win I, if I gain the thing I seek?

—WILLIAM SHAKESPEARE, *THE RAPE OF LUCRECE*

In conclusion, I want to share with you a few lines from a famous piece of literature. As I mentioned earlier, we all seek inner peace. You have learned the Reality Model, read examples, and learned the steps to apply it. In this chapter you will see an example that sums up much of what may go on inside someone's head when he or she thinks about the results of future behavior.

Along with many wonderful and memorable plays, William Shakespeare wrote poetry. One of his poems is titled *The Rape of Lucrece*, and is about a man by the name of Lucius Tarquinius Superbus (535–496 BC) who was the legendary seventh and final king of Rome. In the poem, Lucius is thinking about raping the beautiful Lucrece. And while he is thinking about this ugly, foul deed, these words come into his mind:

What win I, if I gain the thing I seek?
A dream, a breath, a froth of fleeting joy.
Who buys a minute's mirth to wail a week?
Or sells eternity to get a toy?

For one sweet grape who would the vine destroy?
Or what fond beggar, but to touch the crown,
Would with the scepter straight be stricken down?

(lines 211–17)

Think about this Shakespeare poem. It illustrates what we're talking about. What if every time you had to make a decision, for good or for ill, these words came to your mind?

Meeting Your Needs over Time

You may never remember this verse in its entirety, but always remember the first line: "What win I, if I gain the thing I seek?" This is simply another way of asking, Will the results of my behavior meet my needs over time? Shakespeare understood this idea many hundreds of years ago. It is a very old idea. If people understood the power of their beliefs and how those beliefs affect behavior, what kind of decisions would they make? What decisions will you make now that you understand that power?

If you learn nothing more from this book than to start asking yourself this question, to quote the first line of this stanza from *The Rape of Lucrece* to help ground you, it will bring you a step closer to seeing a marked and measurable change in how you make personal and professional decisions. And what if you taught your children this concept of beliefs and perceptions? You'll be changing the course of history.

I should give you an update on the experience I had with JD and the other tough students at the high school, as related in chapter 3. Six weeks after I led that seminar, I got a call from the drug and alcohol specialist for that school district. The first thing out of his mouth was, "What did you do to those kids?"

"What do you mean? I almost didn't survive that."

"Listen," he said, "ten of those kids have completely turned around."

JD was one of them. Eventually JD graduated from high school. Nobody had thought he would. He went to college, he's now married and has a couple of children, and he understands and is teaching his own kids to understand "You are what you believe."

Notes

Chapter 1
Stephen R. Covey.

Chapter 2
Anthony Robbins, *Awaken the Giant Within: How to Take Immediate Control of Your Mental, Emotional, Physical, and Financial Destiny* (New York: Free Press, 1992), 75.

Chapter 3
Steve Maraboli, *Unapologetically You: Reflections on Life and the Human Experience* (Houston: A Better Today, 2013), 73.

Chapter 5
M. Scott Peck, *The Road Less Traveled: A New Psychology of Love, Traditional Values and Spiritual Growth* (New York: Simon and Schuster, 1978), 42.

Chapter 6
Edgar Schein, *Organizational Culture and Leadership* (San Francisco: Jossey-Bass, 2010), 6.

Abraham Maslow, "A Theory of Human Motivation," *Psychological Review* 50 (1943): 370–96.

Stephen R. Covey, *The 8th Habit: From Effectiveness to Greatness* (New York: Free Press, 2004), 22.

Chapter 7
Viktor Frankl, *Man's Search for Meaning* (Boston: Beacon Press, 1946), 112.

Index

About the Author

Hyrum W. Smith is a distinguished author, speaker, and businessman.

For three decades Hyrum has been empowering people to effectively govern their personal and professional lives, combining wit and enthusiasm with a gift for communicating compel-ling principles that incite lasting personal change. His books and presentations have been hailed by audiences in America and internationally.

Hyrum is the author of several nationally acclaimed books, including *The 10 Natural Laws of Successful Time and Life Management* and *What Matters Most.* He also most recently published *The 3 Gaps: Are You Making a Difference?*

In 1984 he became one of the original creators of the popular Franklin Day Planner. He also cofounded the Franklin Quest Company to produce the planner and train individuals and organizations in the time management principles on which the planner was based. He stepped down as chairman and CEO of Franklin Covey Company, Franklin Quest's successor, in 1999; he continued as vice chairman of the board until 2004.

Hyrum has received numerous honors and community service awards, including the following:

- International Entrepreneur of the Year, by Brigham Young University's Marriott School of Management, 1993.
- Three honorary doctorate degrees.
- SRI Gallup Hall of Fame and Man of the Year Award, 1992.
- Silver Beaver Award from the Boy Scouts of America, 1986.

He also serves on several boards of directors and national advisory councils.

After growing up in Honolulu, Hawaii, Hyrum met his wife Gail in London in 1965. They were married in 1966, when Hyrum was on leave from the US Army, where he served as the field commander of a Pershing missile battery in Germany. Upon leaving the army, Hyrum attended Brigham Young University, graduating in 1971.

Hyrum and Gail have had six children (five of whom are living) and twenty-four grandchildren (twenty-two of whom are living).

Hyrum enjoys golfing, shooting pistols and rifles, listening to classical music, horse riding, and spending time with his family at his ranch in southern Utah.

Also by Hyrum W. Smith

The 3 Gaps
Are You Making a Difference?

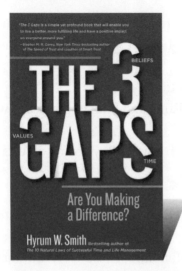

We all want to make a difference. But just as you need to put on your own oxygen mask before helping other passengers on an airplane, getting your own life together is the first step to making a positive impact in the world. Hyrum Smith shows that what stops us are gaps between where we are and where we want to be. The first is the Beliefs Gap, between what we believe to be true and what is actually true. The second is the Values Gap, between what we value most in life and what we actually spend our life doing. The third is the Time Gap, between what we plan to do each day and what we actually get done. This book offers a practical blueprint that we all can use to recognize and close each of these three gaps and illustrates how it can be done through inspiring true stories.

Paperback, 120 pages, ISBN 978-1-62656-662-0
PDF ebook ISBN 978-1-62656-663-7
Digital audio ISBN 978-1-62656-828-0

BK Berrett–Koehler Publishers, Inc.
www.bkconnection.com   800.929.2929

Berrett–Koehler
Publishers

Berrett-Koehler is an independent publisher dedicated to an ambitious mission: *connecting people and ideas to create a world that works for all*.

We believe that to truly create a better world, action is needed at all levels—individual, organizational, and societal. At the individual level, our publications help people align their lives with their values and with their aspirations for a better world. At the organizational level, our publications promote progressive leadership and management practices, socially responsible approaches to business, and humane and effective organizations. At the societal level, our publications advance social and economic justice, shared prosperity, sustainability, and new solutions to national and global issues.

A major theme of our publications is "Opening Up New Space." Berrett-Koehler titles challenge conventional thinking, introduce new ideas, and foster positive change. Their common quest is changing the underlying beliefs, mindsets, institutions, and structures that keep generating the same cycles of problems, no matter who our leaders are or what improvement programs we adopt.

We strive to practice what we preach—to operate our publishing company in line with the ideas in our books. At the core of our approach is stewardship, which we define as a deep sense of responsibility to administer the company for the benefit of all of our "stakeholder" groups: authors, customers, employees, investors, service providers, and the communities and environment around us.

We are grateful to the thousands of readers, authors, and other friends of the company who consider themselves to be part of the "BK Community." We hope that you, too, will join us in our mission.

A BK Life Book

This book is part of our BK Life series. BK Life books change people's lives. They help individuals improve their lives in ways that are beneficial for the families, organizations, communities, nations, and world in which they live and work. To find out more, visit **www.bk-life.com**.

Berrett–Koehler
BK Publishers

Connecting people and ideas
to create a world that works for all

Dear Reader,

Thank you for picking up this book and joining our worldwide community of Berrett-Koehler readers. We share ideas that bring positive change into people's lives, organizations, and society.

To welcome you, we'd like to offer you a free e-book. You can pick from among twelve of our bestselling books by entering the promotional code **BKP92E** here: http://www.bkconnection.com/welcome.

When you claim your free e-book, we'll also send you a copy of our e-newsletter, the *BK Communiqué*. Although you're free to unsubscribe, there are many benefits to sticking around. In every issue of our newsletter you'll find

• A free e-book
• Tips from famous authors
• Discounts on spotlight titles
• Hilarious insider publishing news
• A chance to win a prize for answering a riddle

Best of all, our readers tell us, "Your newsletter is the only one I actually read." So claim your gift today, and please stay in touch!

Sincerely,

Charlotte Ashlock
Steward of the BK Website

Questions? Comments? Contact me at bkcommunity@bkpub.com.

MIX
Paper from
responsible sources
FSC
www.fsc.org   FSC® C011935

Certified

Corporation
bcorporation.net